# REALTALK: THE MAKING OF A MAN

*A story of Life, Lessons and Maturity*

## Eric A. Terry, Sr.

# ACKNOWLEDGMENTS

I thank God for all that He's brought me TO and THROUGH. For every lesson and every blessing. I can do nothing without you. To my wife, Deborah, for being my rock, my inspiration and my one true love. Thank you for loving me beyond the hurt, pain and mistakes of my past. To my kids: Alexis, Eboni, E.J. & Reese. Thank you your love, your laughs, your lessons and for listening. You guys make me proud to be associated with the young adults that you have become. I love you. To my parents: Jerry and Sandra Terry, thank you for your example of what real love looks like. You can stop worrying now. I finally found it. Love you more than life. To My brothers: Kenny and Randy, Thank you for accepting me and for appreciating my differences. I love you guys. To my mentor, my pastor and my friend, Dr. David Banks and First Lady Sylvia: I don't even want to think about where my life would be if it were not for your obedience to the voice of God. Thank you for an investment in my life that has been second to none. To my Empowerment Church Family: Thank you for the "Foot In My Back Ministry."
No one does it better!

To my crew, my band of True Friends: Jordan Slay, Jr., Anagelia Lynch-Brown, Latoya Stevenson, Nate Cox, T.C. Whiteside and Jarrod Dunn. Throughout my life I have been able to call on each of you without hesitation and I thank God for placing each of you in my life for more than just a season. I love you. To my brothers from other mothers, Bobby, Walt, Valitus, Jabari, Derek and Tony. Thank you for always pushing this preacher's kid to walk the path he was designed to take from the beginning. I love you all!!

# INTRODUCTION

My life is full of funny stories, dumb decisions, selfish fights and unnecessary tears. It is also a life full of growth, maturity and freedom. After many years of struggle, I now have the freedom to learn from my own mistakes. I have freedom to admit my wrongs, apologize for them and forgive myself and others. I have the freedom to make better choices in my relationships as well as the freedom from the opinions of others. My freedom came the moment I could be honest with me about me.

To tell you the truth, this was not an easy thing to do. It took some soul searching and just plain old honesty with myself first. I used to lie to myself simply because I could. It didn't begin to harm me until I started to believe my own lies. I call these my "Mirror Moments." It's hard to look yourself in the face and still keep lying. Somebody has to be honest about you. It might as well BE YOU! This book is full of insights I have gained through bad choices, failed decisions in marriage, bad advice and just a few of the lessons I've picked up along the journey to make it all turn out for my good. My purpose in life is to help others navigate their way through difficult periods in their life and relationships to find that place of peace they don't understand but are glad to achieve.

At one point in my life, I thought I could not learn from someone else's failures. I soon realized not only could I learn from their mistakes, but I could learn even more from the things they were now doing successfully. At one of the hardest times in my life, my best friend stopped me in the middle of my "pity party" to tell me something that would change my life forever.

"Failure is ONLY failure if you fail to learn from it."

That hit me like a ton of bricks and my life has not been the same since. Thank you Jordan Slay!

Whether you are single, married, divorced, bitter and angry or just plain numb, it is my prayer this book will help you to see there is a way out of whatever you're in. IT IS POSSIBLE to have a good marriage. IT IS POSSIBLE to break the cycle of failed relationships. IT IS POSSIBLE to have a healthy blended family. IT IS POSSIBLE to live a purpose driven, fulfilled life. Whatever it is you are believing God for, you must first believe that IT IS POSSIBLE!!!

# CONTENTS

## 1 FINDING ME

I came into this world a hefty nine pounds, nine ounces according to my mother. She should know. Lord knows she has reminded me on more than one occasion. I was spoiled rotten from the start. To my paternal grandmother, Dovie Mae Terry, I was the only biological child of her eldest son. This basically meant if I wanted it, all I had to do was point to it. To my God-Mother, Clytie Mae Gresham, I was another chance for her to spoil the fat little baby who lived across the street along with the four older grandchildren that she already had.

These two women gave me the world. I have so many amazing childhood memories of them and I thank God for the impact they had on my life. I'm still amazed at my ability to recall the aroma of their homes from just a simple thought. Thoughts of my grandmother, who passed away when I was twelve years old, can be triggered by the smell of a pot of oatmeal and freshly cooked bacon. Thoughts of my God-Mother remind me of the smell of fried fish and collard greens cooking in her favorite pressure cooker. Other than my mom, these two women made the biggest impacts on me early in life. They taught me to be proud of who I was. They taught me God had a purpose for my life and to use the gifts that He gave me to be a blessing to others.

I was born into an extremely musical family. My influences ranged from the gospel music of Andre Crouch and The Hawkins Family to jazz legends like pianist, Bob James, Thelonious Monk, Joe Sample and my favorite saxophone player, Grover Washington Jr. Music was always a major influence to us. My first exposure to major vocalists came from my own home. Both sets of my grandparents, my mom and dad, my uncles and my middle brother, Randy.

We always joke that my oldest brother, Kenny, was good at a lot of things but singing was just not one of them. I tell people if you glued a note to his back it would slide off. *#GodBlessHim.* I began singing in church at an early age. I couldn't help it. It was all I ever saw. I watched my parents, grandmother and uncles move crowds of people every week. My grandmother with her soul-stirring gospel sound, my mom with her soulful, angelic, soprano voice and my dad and uncle's unmatched harmonies made me think they were all superstars. I wanted to be just like them. Both of my brothers were athletic.

Kenny could run a cross-country marathon and while everyone else was crossing the finish line about to puke, he would look at us like it was nothing and say, "Ya'll ready to go?" It was like he caught a cab and jumped out just before he reached the finish line. I was always amazed at him for that. Kenny is our "Big Toe." The one who keeps us stable. My brother Randy was an all-around all-star.

Football, Basketball and track. He did them all and he was great at every one of them. From being a teammate on a state champion caliber basketball team to defensive player of the week awards on the football field, the dude was good. Most guys were scared of him and most girls wanted to get close to him. These were my big brothers and I couldn't have been more proud of them, but the truth is, I was nothing like either one of them. As a matter of fact, I was their exact opposite. Big, slow, awkward and uninterested in sports or exercise for that matter. Randy tried his best to push me that way, but it's impossible to move a mule when it has no motivation.

One day, after growing tired of being called "Lil Randy," I decided that it was time to make a name for myself and to come out from under the huge shadows cast by my big brothers. Given my size, everyone always asked if I played football too. My answer was always the same, "NOPE!" Now I wanted to do something amazing that would set me apart from both of my brothers' awesome accomplishments. So I went out for football. Did I mention that I wasn't the sharpest crayon in the box at that time either? Out of all of the things I could've chosen, I chose football? Randy's number one sport? *#BigDummy*. Well, it was short lived. After about 45 minutes in the hot sun while wearing a tight helmet and the coach screaming at me to hurry up, I said to myself, "This ain't for me."

I went home mad, depressed and feeling defeated. My dad sat me down and gave me some great advice. "You can't set yourself apart by doing the same thing that they excel in. You're just giving people another area to compare you to your brother." he said. He was right. How stupid! Well, a few years later, at the beginning of my sophomore year at Tyner High School, I finally figured it out. Randy was a senior and headed for college after this school year. Kenny was grown and had his own place at this point. I had to do something now or I would never be rid of their shadows. One day, while sitting in class, my choir director announced that we were having a school talent show. I thought to myself, "That's It!!" Now at this point, I had only sung in church. Most of my friends didn't have a clue that I could sing, but most of them knew that my brother could. Randy had started a group a few years before this. For a moment, I was reluctant to do it, until Randy came to me and said "You can do this! You are a solo singer. You can do it!" Wow! He was really encouraging me to do this, so I did.

The day finally came for me to expose my gift in front of the whole school. I was scared to death. My good friend, Derrick Davis, came to me and asked how I wanted to be introduced. I told him I was doing a song I wrote and this was my first time singing live and this was also the biggest crowd I had ever sung in front of. I thought he was going to laugh dead in my face, but he didn't. He made the introduction and I could hear people in the crowd begin to giggle and murmur, "Eric can't sing." I could feel the butterflies having a fit in my gut. The curtain opened and immediately I heard laughter, but I closed my eyes and pressed past it. My music came on and I opened my mouth and a hush fell over the audience. Students and teachers sat there in shock. All of a sudden, the butterflies were gone and I became someone else for three minutes and thirty five seconds.

Halfway through my song, I looked up into the balcony to see Randy standing to his feet. Proud of his little brother for finally stepping out and finding the one thing that would set him apart. My big brother had just become my biggest cheerleader. As my song came to an end, my schoolmates and teachers stood to their feet and cheered. It was the greatest moment of my life at this point. I did it! I found what Eric was good at and it felt great. Prior to this, I was not the ladies' man that my brothers were. All of a sudden they saw me differently too and I liked it.

After the talent show, I stood at my locker with my best friend, Bobby Hudson. One of the few people who knew that I sang. He was proud of me. He couldn't believe I did it. All of a sudden, I get a tap on my shoulder. It was a girl from my brother's senior class. Her name was Shawn. One of my biggest crushes. She was gorgeous. Bright yellow skin, big gorgeous eyes and she now had her hand placed on my back. As I turned around she says, "Eric, I didn't know you could sing! You have a beautiful voice!" To which I replied with something that sounded like it was straight out of Daffy Duck and Elmer Fudd's illegitimate child's book of pickup lines. She smiled and said, "Aww. That's cute." She giggled and walked off. I wanted to die. Bobby looked at me like "REALLY DUDE?" I had completed the task of making a name for myself and making a complete idiot of myself all within the same hour, but I wouldn't have changed a thing. Now people saw Randy and said "That's Eric's brother." It was a great feeling! Finally! I was no longer under the shadow of my big brothers. I had established a name for myself. I spent the remainder of my high school years in a pretty good place. I had a good core of friends and people around me  I felt that I could really trust. In a lot of ways, I still felt awkward. At this same time, I was feeling the call of God into the ministry.

Now, my father began preaching when I was 7 and he began pastoring his first church when I was 10. This was not something I wanted for myself. It was bad enough being labeled as the "preacher's kid" or "choir boy," but Preaching? NO! I did everything I could to NOT look like that kid. I wanted my friends to see me different. I wanted to be hard. A thug. Why not? It seemed as though that was what every girl my age wanted. It just didn't work for me. I couldn't pull it off.

I saw myself as an outcast seeing that I was so different from everyone else, or so it seemed. While my friends were buying Run-DMC and LL Cool J rap music, I was buying Jazz albums and racing my brothers in the house every day to get control of the TV so I could watch The Carol Burnett Show.

When it came to girls, I was a big chicken. Scared to say anything for fear that I would get rejected in a major way. I had a lot of crushes, but was too afraid to tell anyone about them until we were grown. I was six foot three and over three hundred pounds by the time I was fifteen years old. In my mind, all of the girls I liked wanted the skinny guys with all of the athletic abilities. No one wanted to date the fat dude, even if he could sing, so I thought. As I look back on that, I used to have major regrets because I felt like I missed out on a few possible relationships, but even more so, I missed out on some even better friendships.

I was a different kid. When I was on stage, I had all of the confidence in the world. I would walk off of the stage, walk right to the most attractive woman on the front row and take her by the hand and sing directly to her and sweep her off her feet. The moment the show was over, I turned back into the big shy kid afraid to talk to women. You could find me cowering in the dressing room or sitting out in the car. My brother and the other guys were just the opposite. They had no problem approaching girls. I literally got sick to my stomach just from the thought of being laughed at or just flat out rejected by a beautiful woman in a public setting.

I remember being in the mall one time with my brother, Randy, and we saw some girls who recognized us from our recent show on their college campus. Randy and the other guys went to talk to them while I hid behind a store sign. Man, I was a big punk! I simply allowed fear to keep me from reaching out to someone who just might have seen me in a different light. I let fear tell me that it was impossible for a beautiful young lady to be interested in someone like me.

In the summer leading up to my senior year of high school, I worked really hard in my music career while working a nine-to-five job at Arby's restaurant. My brother and I lived in Marietta, GA and we didn't have a car at the time, so we walked everywhere we went. We walked to work, the mall, to the pool, and to friend's houses. It was great to be able to buy my own clothes and pay for things I wanted, and I was gaining a little confidence along the way. I didn't realize it until I got back home to Chattanooga for my senior year, but I had lost a ton of weight and felt good about myself. I bought my own school clothes that year. I wanted to finish my final year of high school with a new attitude and a new look. I got my ear pierced and dressed as clean cut as I could. You couldn't tell me that I didn't look good. When my friends saw me, they were amazed at the new look and style. My goal was to make my last year my best year. As far as my love life, I had recently had a break up with my girlfriend of almost two years. You'll hear more about that later. I was ready for a change. On the first day of school, I walked into my English class trying to find my seat. My teacher had me sitting right up front. Man, I hated that…until this gorgeous young lady walked into the classroom. She was new to the school and the teacher pointed her to the desk directly behind me. I thought she was the most beautiful thing I had ever seen, but of course, I was too shy and too scared to say anything to her. The funny part was, I had to talk to her every single day. The teacher would have us passing paperwork back and forth.

We sometimes graded each other's class work and of course this made me a nervous wreck. After getting to know her, I found out that we shared the same birthday. This made me like her even more. I wanted to ask her out to celebrate our birthdays so badly, but fear said, "Don't be a fool and embarrass yourself! She doesn't want to be seen out anywhere with you!" I think she knew that I liked her from the start, but she never said a word, nor did she embarrass me by exposing me to everyone else. She just looked at me and smiled every single day and I loved it.

My crush became our little secret. We became really good friends but for years I wondered what if. What if I had actually told her how I felt? I wonder what she might have said. I wondered if she felt the same way about me. Could it be possible? Just maybe she was just as fearful as I was. Nah…she was too fine for that. I told myself that it was impossible for her to want anything more with me other than friendship. She could have her choice of any guy in the school. What could she possibly see in me? Unfortunately, those questions and many more went unanswered for me. I allowed fear to control my life in such a major way for most of my childhood and a good part of my adult life. So here are a few questions for you. How do you handle the fears in your own life? Do you allow them to keep you from doing the things that you might enjoy? Do you let fear tell you that you're not worthy of certain types of relationships because of your past or because of what YOU see in the mirror? Do you stay in bad relationships because you've convinced yourself that this is as good as it gets? I did this for a long time, but soon, fear had to take a back seat.

*Interested in booking Eric for speaking engagements, marriage conferences, retreats or singles events?*
*Go to www.realtalkconsultants.com today.*

## 2 MY FLESH, MY PAST MY GOD!

During my high school years, I joined the singing group my brother Randy started with some friends when he was in junior high school. We began doing small venues in Atlanta, Muscle Shoals, AL and several other places and even some recording. We had a blast and made pretty good money doing it. Soon after graduation, I moved to Atlanta to be with the rest of the group. College was the farthest thing from my mind. It was music or nothing. I was soon presented the chance of a lifetime.

My dad had a good friend who was the president of Morehouse College in Atlanta. They were trying to give me a full ride. What an amazing opportunity this was. Too bad I was too focused on my music to take them up on it. I let it slip through my fingers because I saw myself doing nothing else but music. Soon after that, our music career came to an abrupt end when our drummer and keyboard player left the group and our manager stole some of our music and sold it to a few major record labels with his name on the copyright papers instead of ours. This was a major blow. The very thing I had worked so hard for was gone. My dream of being a major artist was over. Devastated, I moved back home and Randy and my cousin, Aaron, decided to move to Houston, TX with some of our other family. I began a cycle of working jobs that I hated, but needed.

About a year later, I met a young lady who I thought was very attractive, But I assumed there was no way she would be interested in me. My cousin, Latoya, threw a party and asked me and my best friend, Daymonn Carson to DJ for her. **(Rest In Peace, Day)** Guess who was there. She walked in and I was done. Some call it love at first sight, others simply call it, "Horny seventeen year old boy meets sexy older woman." Whatever it was, I had it. After the party, we began to talk pretty regularly. After a few dates and dinners at her house, we were a couple. By the way, I mentioned that she was older but I failed to disclose the age difference. I was 17. She was 21, divorced with 3 very small children and I thought I was head over hills in love with her and no one could tell me any different. I grew attached to the kids really quickly, especially the two youngest boys. Her beautiful older daughter became my little princess. I took them everywhere with me.

As I look back, I can't help but wonder what everyone else was thinking. No one was saying a word to me about our relationship. I was 17 years old for God's sake! No matter, we were together and soon we began the planning stages of our wedding. Yep! I said wedding. We went all out. Decorated my dad's church and had plenty of friends and family there to witness this special occasion. It was a beautiful ceremony. As we walked out of the church headed for our reception, my new bride threw up her hand to wave at someone as we got into the limo. All of a sudden, the wedding ring that I had just placed on her finger went flying down the street and into a drainage ditch. Hmmm. It wasn't a good fit. What a surprise. We truly should have taken this as an omen, but of course we didn't. After searching the tall grass near my father's church and digging in the drain, we found it and moved forward to dance the night away and begin our new life together.

We didn't see it at the time, but our marriage was doomed from the start. Nothing went right. We argued over everything and didn't see eye to eye on anything except sex. Let's be real for a minute. I was seventeen years old. I had very little sexual experience so any sex was great to me. After a little over a year of being together, I just didn't feel right. I felt as if something was wrong. We still had the same arguments and our sex life was about the same, but something was different. I felt like I was missing something but I just couldn't put my finger on it. Slowly, we became more distant. She would leave the house for extremely long periods of time and tell me that she was visiting her grandmother. Through it all, I was determined to make it work the same way that my parents did. One day my friend Paul picked me up and took me for a ride. My wife was gone to visit her grandmother who lived across town. I didn't go with her because I was recovering from the flu.

Paul said there was something he needed me to see. I realized that he was not going to let this go, so I went. We drove down a little street not too far from our home. He began to slow down as we approached a house that he wanted me to see so desperately. As we drove a little further, I looked up and see my wife on the porch of this house. She is dressed in a totally different set of clothes than she left with and she's sitting on the lap of another man. I was floored. I had Paul take me back home and I packed my things and went to my parents. I didn't know what to do. I went home, pissed off like never before. I wasn't prepared for this, but I knew that I couldn't continue like this. We went back and forth for a while about working it out, but in my heart I knew that it was never meant to be in the first place. It was over, but neither of us wanted to come out of our own pocket to pay for the divorce so we remained separated for a couple of years.

Meanwhile, I moved back to my parent's house feeling like a complete failure.

I remember having a conversation with my mom one day. I told her I didn't understand what happened. I had done what they had always taught us and prayed about it. My mom looked at me and said, "I believe you prayed, but my question is did you listen to what God was trying to tell you?" Talk about a shot to the kidneys. I was not ready for that question, but it was true. I hadn't listened. I allowed my flesh to lead me into a place that God never meant for me to be in the first place. Believe me when I tell you, you will always stay longer than you want to stay when you go to a place God never intended for you go.

Not knowing how to heal from past hurts, I thought the best way to get over one relationship was to get into another one. I couldn't have been more wrong. After my first failed marriage at 19 years old, I tried to move on but really didn't know how. I tried dating other girls my age but they all seemed to fall apart before they got going good. I began trying to date the cousin of a girl my brother was seeing. We were great together. We had a lot in common. We laughed, played and cried together and I really thought, maybe, just maybe she might be "The One." I would go to her house and fix dinner and help her look after her baby boy from a previous relationship. We were never physical with one another. At nineteen and previously sexually active, this was driving me nuts, but I saw it as a good thing. Seeing that I went into my first marriage with nothing but sex on the brain, maybe this was a good thing. I couldn't let something like that ruin this one, so I kept my cool and just tried to make the best of our relationship without it. Of course, I knew that this was God's way, anyway.

One day I attempted to make it official with her. Not a proposal, but just to be able to say that we were dating exclusively. She told me she couldn't do it. She told me I was too sweet. Too nice. What the hell? Are you serious? Too nice? What in the hell does that even mean? She told me that I was the man of her dreams, but I deserved better and she wanted me to find someone who would treat me the way I deserved. I was done. I didn't that my heart could take much more of this. Another relationship gone. This time because of the fears she had in moving forward with a "Good guy." She had allowed fear to tell her she wasn't good enough for me. Me? The guy that was still trying to recover from a divorce at 19? WOW! So once again, I was alone and hurt. This was a place that was becoming all too familiar to me at a really early age. I was beginning to get too afraid to share my feelings for anyone. Maybe it was me. What was I doing wrong? I just wanted the same thing I saw my parents build but for some reason, it continued to elude my grasp. I tried to move on, but in the back of my mind, the only way I knew to fix this was another relationship. So my journey continued for Mrs. Right.

About a year later, I got a call from my mom telling me the grandfather of an ex-girlfriend had passed away. Remember the girlfriend I mentioned I dated for over a year in high school? Although it had been 4 years since we had spoken, I was close to her grandfather and truly sorry to hear about her family's loss. She was living out of town in college at the time and would be going back to school soon after the funeral. I remembered her grandmother's address and wrote her a letter to express my condolences. In my letter, I asked her to please give me a call if she felt up to it. She did. She received my letter on the day after the funeral as she was heading back to school. We exchanged phone numbers and promised to keep in touch. This was January of 1994 and by April of that year, I was moving to Nashville to be closer to her. I immediately found a job and we started working to rekindle the relationship we had in high school for almost two years. I found myself back with my high school sweetheart and I was loving it. I thought just maybe we could get back to what we had before we went our separate ways several years before. We were growing closer but it was too much way too fast and we couldn't see it.

A short while later, at 21 years old, my girlfriend awakened me from a nap to tell me that I was going to be a father. I was ecstatic! We had recently had a conversation and made the decision to become parents but I don't think that either of us ever dreamed that it would happen this fast. There we were, not much more than kids ourselves with absolutely no child rearing experience. A mom and dad. What in the hell was I thinking? I wasn't prepared to be anyone's father but of course I didn't stop there with my decisions. Three weeks' after the birth of our beautiful daughter, Alexis, we made the decision to become husband and wife. Don't get me wrong, becoming a father and a husband weren't necessarily bad decisions, it was just bad timing.

> "Preparation is KEY to doing anything effectively."

Preparation is key to doing anything effectively and we were not prepared for either role. So what would our marriage look like? What should we expect? How would we interact? These were questions that neither of us had answers too. We both brought our own ideas but we really didn't know how any of this was going to work. Imagine this: She began living with her grandparents at the age of four. Her father was around in spurts, so the only positive male in her life was her grandfather who she grew to love and cherish. He was a hard worker and a loving man. Her grandmother was old school. What she said was law. She was strict and a times this shifted over into something else altogether. She was about business. She made sure that the house ran like a well-oiled machine, but she didn't play.

My new wife's grandparent's relationship was more about a partnership than a relationship. They worked well together. We know that they had their issues in their earlier years, but they were at a good place when she came along. He made the money while she managed it. He provided a house and she made it a home. What a great partnership. Although there was a limited amount of affection towards one another, they gave their granddaughter all the love they knew how. Then there's my story. Raised with both parents in the home. My mother was previously in an abusive relationship. Once she got out, she was determined not to go through that again. So when she met my dad, she's brought two little knuckleheaded boys with her. My dad was a "church boy." He didn't really have much choice. My grandmother didn't play either. He knew how to serve people. He brought those same skills into his marriage by serving his wife and the two boys that he now laid claim too. About 9 months later, I hit the scene and completed the group. We were raised in a home full of love and affection. We saw them hug, kiss, hold hands and just all around love. Not only for one another, but they were equally loving for the three of us as well. Theirs was a partnership, but of a different sort. They worked well together. They both worked full-time jobs.

My mom was the main caretaker of the house and the kids, but they managed our home as a team. The only shared house chores were divided between my brothers and I. My dad didn't do a lot of that other than cooking on his off days. My parents were great together. They still are after almost 43 years. They talked, they cried, they disagreed, but we never knew it. After we were all grown, my brothers and I talked about how cool it was to grow up in a house where we saw real love and never even heard our parents even raise their voices at one another. That's right, not even once.

About a year ago, I interviewed my dad and I asked him how they did it. He simply said. "Son, it was a choice that we made. We didn't want to involve you boys in something that you had no control over." I was in awe at his response. "A Choice." Wow! A simple decision that they stuck to. Then I asked him the ultimate question; "How does it feel to be married for over 40 years with a wonderful relationship but have three sons who had all struggled through their own divorces?" He was stunned. A quiet fell over the room.

He had never thought of it that way.

Needless to say, at 22 years old, my new wife and I had our work cut out for us. We had no idea that the biggest hurdle we would face was our own expectations. She expected our house to run like the house she was raised in and I expected our house to run like the house that I was raised in. Only one problem with this; we went into our marriage with two separate thoughts. Two sets of expectations. Two different visions and we never once sat down and discussed this. So with a three week old baby girl and no real guidance or counseling on how to navigate through this journey, we were off. Later that year, I began to feel a strong pull on my spirit. I realized that God was once again reminding me of the calling to preach the Gospel I had been running from for some years now. I couldn't run any longer. On October 29, 1995, I delivered my first sermon at the Lake Providence Baptist Church in Nashville, TN under the leadership of Pastor H. Bruce Maxwell.

We were in a good place. Within a month, we moved back to our hometown for new job opportunities and to raise our little family. I soon realized trying to raise a child in the same house with the man and woman who raised me was not the easiest thing to do. When I tried to be the strict parent, they played the sensitive grandparents. We were bumping heads and it was not working for me or my new bride. We soon moved out and got our own place. It was the ugliest, most run-down little duplex that you could ever imagine.

We pulled up to see it for the first time and I wanted to laugh, but at the same time I thought to myself, do you really want to continue to stay in your parent's house right now? I heard a resounding NO in my spirit. This place was a dump! It was a bright, dirty, Pepto-Bismol shade of pink with a sloped, rocky, dirt driveway. The backyard looked like a jungle and it looked like a former but recent crack house. I turned to my wife who in turn, looked at me and said, "It's nice." Maybe she was looking at the house next door. Nope, I quickly interpreted that as "I'll take it because we need to get out of your mama's house." I agreed and we paid our deposit, packed up and moved in a few days later.

It wasn't long before we began to have our own problems. What was an "ok" friendship at first was now becoming a nightly battle. Life was taking place and we were not prepared for it. Bills, money issues, parenting concerns, a lack of communication and constant bickering began to rule our once happily rekindled relationship. About three years later, my wife comes and says, "I'm pregnant." Now we were about to bring another baby into our jacked up relationship and we didn't have a clue on how to fix it. We were talking to everyone but each other.

Our expectations grew further and further apart and we saw eye to eye on nothing. We were growing more distant. I was not ready for either of the roles I had taken on, but it was too late. To add insult to injury, I had already allowed my flesh to control me. Yeah, the young preacher man had strayed from his marriage. I didn't feel I was getting everything that I needed from my wife. Looking back, I'm sure she wasn't getting everything she needed from me. Walking in my flesh and emotions caused me to search outside my marriage. I found someone who listened. Someone who encouraged me and who made me feel like a man although at the time, I didn't really have a true understanding of what that meant. She trusted me and we leaned on each other. I was falling apart spiritually. I knew what I was doing was wrong, but I couldn't seem to stop. Truth is, I was making a decision not to stop.

Our relationship didn't start out this way. In the beginning, it was truly innocent, but the more we talked, the closer we got and the more emotionally attached we became. Being with someone who lifts you up when everything else constantly tells you that you're a failure, is a hard thing to let go of when it's providing the very thing that you crave the most. Here I was trying to do ministry to bless others. Preaching, praying, leading praise & worship all over the place, but meanwhile, my own life was a wreck and I was slowly dying inside. I felt more spiritually detached than I ever had before. I was doing everything I could to keep my family together, except the things I needed to do to make it right.

I was there physically and handled things as best I could financially, but I was too immature and caught up in my flesh to recognize that I needed help. I needed to talk to someone who could give me some guidance but after my first marriage ended in divorce, I was determined NOT to take advice from anyone who had experienced divorce. This was one of the dumbest mistakes I could have made. Eventually, I chose to sit down and talk to my father. My parents didn't know a lot about what was going on between my wife and I. They taught my brothers and me, "What goes on in your house stays in your house," but I needed help fast. So I sat down with my dad and began to tell him all of the issues that we were experiencing. He was stunned. Everything seemed perfect in their eyes and for the first time in my life, the father I could go to with any question looked at me and simply said, "Just pray, Son." I was amazed. "Is that all you've got?" Prayer? That's it? We had both been praying, now we wanted to punch each other in the throat! NOW WHAT? My problem was, I failed to realize my prayers were hindered by the very actions that led me to this point in my life.

My dad had no idea what else to tell me. I remember leaving the house that day even angrier than I was when I was talking to him, but now my anger was directed towards him. Why didn't he have more to say? Why couldn't he help me with this? He was supposed to have all of the answers, but he didn't. I was upset with my dad for a long time until God really arrested me one day. I heard the spirit ask me this question. "How is your dad supposed to teach you something that he has never experienced himself?" It's like calling your auto mechanic and asking him to build a house. He couldn't help me with something that he hadn't been through. So things continued as they were. All the time getting worse. We grew further and further apart. We tried to continue, but as the years passed, she grew tired and I grew distant. How could we get past this? Why didn't we see this coming? How could we get back to the high school sweetheart status that we once shared? We had no clue and we grew more and more frustrated. After almost 10 years of marriage, it was over.

I was a mess and my family was gone. I was thirty two years old and my second marriage had just ended in divorce. My spiritual life was falling apart and I felt like my life itself was crumbling around me. I was depressed, emotionally unstable and suicidal. I was at a point where I found myself wanting to end it all and just be done, BUT GOD. As I was driving to church one day, my eyes full of tears and my heart broken, I began to ask God, "Why?" Why was I going through this? Why had I failed once again? Why could I not make my marriage work? How was anyone going to be able to receive ministry from me after two failed marriages?

In the middle of my crying. In the middle of self-pity, I heard the Spirit of God clearly say to me, **"You chose your first wife out of your flesh. You chose your second wife trying to relive your past. Let me choose your next wife and I'll give you the helpmate that I designed for your future."** I knew I had to make some changes. In order for me to be prepared for what God had destined for my life, I had to get rid of some baggage. I had to get to a level of maturity I personally had not reached. I could not go into another relationship with the same mess I had been carrying around for the last 12 plus years. Basically, I needed to grow up. I needed to acknowledge and change my selfish ways. I had to acknowledge that being "vengeful" in order to "Get back" at anyone who I felt had wronged me had to go away.

My friend Jordan once told me, "Two wrongs don't make it right, E." I was in such a selfish place at the time, I replied, "Maybe not, Jay, but it damn sho' makes us even." *#Ridiculous*. Enough was enough. I had to make some changes. It was also at this point that my good friend shared the words of wisdom that would change my whole perspective on life. ***"Failure is only failure when you fail to learn from it."*** These words sparked something in my spirit. It was a reminder that my failure wasn't final. It let me know that failing did not make me a failure. My decisions did not define who I was, but I had to be willing to change if I wanted anything else to change.

## KEYS TO REMEMBER:

- Preparation is key to doing anything effectively
- Failure is only failure if you fail to learn from it
- Allow God to direct your relationship path instead of your flesh

*Interested in booking Eric for speaking engagements, marriage conferences, retreats or singles events?*
*Go to www.realtalkconsultants.com today.*

## 3 A CHANCE FOR CHANGE

Ask yourself this question, "How well do I handle change?" Most people will say it depends on the type of change. The truth is, change will come whether we are ready to accept it or not. After two marriages that ended in divorce, a now damaged relationship with my parents and a spiritual life that was so out of place, I was lost. I had no idea how to begin the process of getting any of it back. I had come to a point in my life that I was tired and truly ready for something to change, and I realized it had to begin with me. It wasn't easy, but I had to take a look at my part in all of the mess I called my life.

Whether it was good, bad or ugly, it was mine, so where do I begin? I first had to start by getting over what other people thought, said or felt. I had no power to change how they felt towards me, but I could change the way I responded to it. To start, I had to look at the situation with my parents. We always had such a great relationship. They were always there to help lead and direct me in everything aspect of my life, but in the midst of all of this, I found myself living the life that they desired for me, but it wasn't truly what I wanted. After my second divorce, my relationship with my parents began to change for the worse. I felt that I could no longer go to them, mostly because of their close relationship with my ex-wife.

Shortly after we separated, my ex and my two kids moved in with my parents. This was a hard pill to swallow. Here I was staying on the living room floor of a friend's one bedroom apartment, but my ex was living in the house that I grew up in. Going to visit my parents became difficult. Holidays were unbearable. I felt like I couldn't truly have a relationship with them because of their relationship with her. I wasn't upset that they had a relationship with her. I just felt like it went a little beyond the scope of an "ex" mother and father in law. She was becoming the daughter they never had and I was feeling like less than their son. One day I went to visit them when I thought she was gone. While talking to my parents, I began to look around and notice where there were once pictures of the sons they raised, there were now pictures of my kids and my ex. Of course I expected to see the pictures of the kids. That was normal, but to see more pictures of my ex than me and my brothers? This bothered me. While talking to them, I mentioned this to my mom and dad. They were stunned. I honestly don't think that they even realized it, but if someone who didn't know walked into their home, they would be under the impression that they had one daughter and two grandchildren instead of three sons and four grandchildren.

After making this known, it took me a while to visit again. When I did, I remember my dad making a point to show me a picture that was now placed on one of the end tables. It was a picture of my dad, myself and my son, EJ from a few years earlier. I knew that it wasn't there before. As a matter of fact, it was dusty like it had been in a closet or under a table for some time. It had fresh fingerprints on it from where they had recently put it on display. I wasn't impressed. It actually made me angrier rather than resolved how I was feeling.

My relationship with them was becoming more difficult to deal with. I felt like they had chosen her over me. They didn't call to see how I was doing or if I needed anything, yet my ex had all of their support and was floating between the homes of my parents and my grandmother who stayed right next door. I felt as if everyone was against me. She had the support I should've had from them. I would visit them and I felt like I was the former in-law instead of the son. I had already lost my wife and kids, now I felt like I was losing my relationship with the only family I had. This was MY family. Why was she still here? Why couldn't she go to HER family? These were the questions I began to ask myself. Yeah, it may have seemed awkward and out of place, but it was quickly becoming my new normal. I never wanted to be a "weekend dad." I didn't know how to do that. After the divorce, it just got worse. My ex and I had no idea how to communicate with one another. Every conversation turned into an argument. We couldn't make any decisions without fighting about it. I never wanted this for my kids. They deserved to grow up just like I did in a peaceful home where the parents worked it out without involving them, but that clearly wasn't our reality.

Before the divorce, I became very vengeful and spiteful to my wife. Just the opposite of how I saw my father interact with my mom. I had become someone I didn't recognize and it did not help our situation after the divorce. I became more and more bitter. Great qualities for the preacher man, huh? I had to change. No matter what someone else did or said, it was in this season of my life I learned everything depended on how I responded to the things that happened in my life.

For the first time in my life, I was living completely on my own. After sleeping on my friend's floor for a while, I had finally saved enough money for the deposit on my own place. This was new territory for me. In my past, I had gone from growing up in my parent's home to sharing a house with my brother and bandmates, back to my parent's house. From there, I had a roommate for a short period then I moved in with my girlfriend turned wife in Nashville. I had never lived on my own and I was scared to death. I was used to giving someone the money for bills and trusting them to take care of it, but now, it was all on me. Bills, food, car maintenance, etc. It was all on me.

I moved into my small, one bedroom apartment with pride. It was the most pitiful thing you could ever imagine. It was a nice place, but I had absolutely nothing to go in it. I bought a new bed from one of the hotels going out of business but didn't have a frame. I literally put my new King-sized bed and box springs on the floor and kept it moving. No TV, no cookware. Nothing. When I moved out, the only thing I took was my pillow. I borrowed sheets for a make-shift bed when I got to my friend Gary's place. I had recently found a job working third shift as a payday loan supervisor. My employees were the best. When they found out about my apartment, I showed up at work one night to find that they had planned a shower for me to help furnish my apartment. It was amazing! They bought everything from curtains to pictures and other decorations. Soon, even my ex-wife got in on the furnishing of my place.

Out of the blue, she called me one day to ask if I wanted the old couch, loveseat and chair from our home. She had it all in storage and really didn't want it anymore and she didn't want to continue to pay the storage fees. I was shocked but grateful. As we continued to converse, she told me that I could have it all. Furniture, Televisions, lamps, etc. Once again, I was grateful, but wondered where this graciousness was coming from. Meanwhile, I furnished my new place. I was proud of my little bachelor pad. My goal was to make it look and feel like my Uncle Charlie's place. He was my dad's middle brother and the ultimate bachelor. He was another big influence on me when it came to music, especially Jazz.

Though he never married, there was no shortage of women in his life. My uncle was a player and my brothers and I were impressed. When you came into my place, I wanted the atmosphere to be smooth, elegant and jazzy. I did what I could with my Goodwill furniture and Family Dollar decorations. You couldn't tell me a thing. It was "MY" place. My kids loved coming over. For that short time, we were able to go back to the way things were before the divorce. They were only nine and five at the time of the divorce. We played games, watched all of their favorite movies and the evening always ended with me chasing them through the house with the "Tickle Monster" that seemed to attach itself to my wrist whenever they were nearby. I loved it but I hated taking them back to their mom's. I hated the feeling of going back to an empty house alone. No kid's laughter and no Barney and Disney songs driving me nuts. Just me. It wasn't supposed to be like this, but it was my reality and I had been the key factor in where we were at this point. Something had to change and it had to begin with me. I was determined that I would always be a part of my kid's lives. I had seen guys distance themselves from the kids because of their relationship with the kid's mom. I didn't want this. I wanted my babies.

One day while sitting in my apartment, I had a "Mirror Moment" conversation with myself. I began to ask myself some really difficult questions. What was your part in all of this? Why did you go against the very thing you saw and admired in your parents? What made you so combative with your wife? Why were you so angry? It was only then I realized I was simply doing what a lot of men do when they feel that the world is against them and they can't win. I got mad and lashed out at whoever was closest to me. I wasn't even an argumentative person. To be honest, I hated conflict, but yet I found myself right in the middle of it and in most cases, initiating that very thing I hated the most.

While in the process of this daily conversation with myself, I got a call from the loan company where I got my car. They were calling to tell me that my ex-wife had just paid off the balance on my car. WHAT?!? I was floored. Although I was having these monumental conversations with myself, I still was not treating her any better, yet she just paid off the car that was still in both of our names. I didn't know how to respond. The sad thing is, I was too mad, prideful and pigheaded to even call her and say thank you. Two simple words that I expected from her at every turn, yet it took me years to be able to say it to her. That's what pride and stupidity will get you. We slowly began to be able to talk without fighting. We were both moving on with our separate lives while doing everything that we could to keep our kids as the center. One day, my ex-wife called me and began to apologize for her part in all of the things we had been through over the years. I held the other end of the phone in sheer shock. Eventually, I couldn't allow her to be the only person who was confessing and admitting wrongdoing in our marriage. It was a joint screw-up and I had the biggest role. This was by far one of our best conversations in years. Just simple forgiveness in its purest form. It was cleansing for us both.

A little while after this, my daughter had begun having problems in school and at home. She was fine with me but she was becoming a terror with her mom and anyone else in authority. I knew the divorce was hard on her, but we didn't understand where all of this was coming from. After several major blow ups, I sat her down one day to have a long talk about what was going on. Eventually, she admitted to being mad at her mom. When I asked her why, she said, "Mommy is the reason you left!" I was floored. I never spoke negative to either of my kids about their mom, so where was this coming from? She then tells me she heard the conversation her mom and I were having the day she called and apologized. I felt like a huge failure. I wanted to cry. My daughter was acting out because I wasn't in the house and she blamed her mom for it. Great job, Dad.

As she sat there with tears in her eyes, bitter, angry and upset, I just held her and let her know she had only heard one side of a two-sided conversation. Yes, she heard her mom apologizing to me, but what she didn't heard was my apologies to her. It wasn't just her mom's fault. The blame belonged to both of us, but especially me as the head of the house. I was afraid this would change my relationship with my daughter, but I trusted God and told her the truth. It was on me.

I then began to teach her something I had learned throughout this process. *"It's not what happens to us, but it's how we respond that makes the difference."* I found myself repeating this to her as well as myself on a daily basis. It started to change how I saw a lot of things. I now had to examine my own actions concerning everything that had ever happened to me in my life. The kids who picked on me about my weight. The girls who I assumed would laugh in my face and reject me for liking them. The preacher/manager who stole music from my brother and I as teenagers, halting my music career. My first ex-wife who cheated on me. My second ex-wife who I felt never truly respected me as a man when I never really acted like one. My parents who I felt had replaced me with their relationship with my ex-wife. I had to examine every aspect of my life and look at how I could have handled every situation differently in an attempt for a better outcome. When I finished looking at it all, I came to the understanding that I had done what I considered at this point to be a laughably piss-poor and pitiful job of handling my relationships. To sum it all up, I saw myself as a big, fat failure. All of a sudden, the words of my friend came once again to encourage me. ***"Failure is only failure when you fail to learn from it."*** This phrase was slowly becoming my new mantra. It would be years later when I realized why this was so important.

As a man, my number one need over sex, food or shelter is SUCCESS. Any place a man does not feel successful, he sees himself as a failure. Therefore, he has no drive, no ambition and no goals without first seeing some area of success in his life. No matter what area of life we're talking about, the success of a man is what drives him. It's what gives him purpose. It's the thing that gives him peace. So with this new revelation, I had the task of rebuilding Eric, The Man. I had to forgive myself and others who I felt had a hand in the scenarios in my life. I had to get back to God and stop trusting so much in myself to get this thing together. I had to find out my purpose in life and focus on it. It all sounded really good, but I had no clue as to where to even start. In all of this time, I continued to do ministry.

Preaching, singing and ministering to people who were hurting, confused and faithless. I learned to be a good supporter and servant to the people, but I was still unable to serve the people closest to me in the ways that I needed to because I hadn't found a way to rid myself of the pain I was feeling. Some may ask, how do you minister to the hurt others are experiencing when you are dealing with the same thing? First, I learned that people who have been through the most have the potential to give the

> **"I could only help someone else if I was able to come from a place of wisdom and forgiveness instead of a place of bitterness and defeat."**

best advice. Since I was dealing with a lot of these things myself, I could only help someone else if I was able to come from a place of wisdom and forgiveness instead of a place of bitterness and defeat. Seeking help from someone who has gone through the same thing you have is not a bad thing, but you must make sure they can advise you from a place of peace and success instead of one of pain. Unfortunately, there were times when my ministry was merely ineffective smoke and mirrors seeing that I was ministering in a place of bitterness.

The cycle had to stop. I wasn't able to move forward at all. I was simply moving around in a circle and going nowhere. I had to get it together in order for me to walk into what God had planned for me. Remember the promise he made to me about allowing Him to choose my next wife? I had to give him total control in order to receive the very thing He had promised me after my second divorce. I had to allow him to be Lord over every aspect of my life to truly see His power operate in my life. I knew it would not be an easy road, but I also had no idea of the obstacles or the blessings that I would encounter along the way.

*Interested in booking Eric for speaking engagements, marriage conferences, retreats or singles events?*
*Go to www.realtalkconsultants.com today.*

# 4 PLAYING OUT OF POSITION

In my quest to become the man I wanted to be, needed to be and that God designed me to be, I had to acknowledge that was out of position in the first place. I had to acknowledge that I was a liar, cheater and needed some major help. I'll be honest with you, this was a difficult thing to do. Pride, ego and all of the things that most people think makes a man a man had to be dropped immediately. I had to put pride aside and get real with myself for once. This was the only way I would ever be able to get myself back on point if I wanted help others to recognize and make the changes necessary for their own lives.

I had to go back to the beginning. Not my beginning, but the beginning of man. I started a bible study group called KLS "Kingdom Living Study." The focus of this group was to examine the myths and the lies that religion had taught us as children. One of the first bible stories we looked at was Adam and Eve. This story wasn't just the beginning of the bible, but it was

MY beginning. Don't zone out because of the bible verses. I promise you I'm going somewhere with this. Stay with me, I'm gonna bless ya! Let's look at what I found that helped me in my personal life regarding my relationships.

## The First Man
### Genesis 2:4-9 (New Century Version)

*4 This is the story of the creation of the sky and the earth. When the Lord God first made the earth and the sky,*

*5 there were still no plants on the earth. Nothing was growing in the fields because the Lord God had not yet made it rain on the land. And there was no person to care for the ground,*

*6 but a mist would rise up from the earth and water all the ground.*

*7 Then the Lord God took dust from the ground and formed a man from it. He breathed the breath of life into the man's nose, and the man became a living person.*

*8 Then the Lord God planted a garden in the east, in a place called Eden, and put the man he had formed into it.*

*9 The Lord God caused every beautiful tree and every tree that was good for food to grow out of the ground. In the middle of the garden, God put the tree that gives life and also the tree that gives the knowledge of good and evil.*

The previous 6 verses of scripture are the key to the entire basis for what I realized my problem was as well as the problem with most men in the world today. It's all about our ORIGINAL POSITION. Notice that even before God created Adam, He had a PURPOSE for his existence. He had a PLAN for his life. He had a POSITION created just for him. Adam was the overseer of the earth that God had created before his own existence. He was to rule and have complete dominion over it. The verses that follow give us a more in depth look at what God created and the instructions He gave to Adam. His job description. We see Adam's original position, now let's fast forward a bit and take a look at where he got out of position.

## The First Relationship
### Genesis 2:18-24 (New Century Version)

*18 Then the Lord God said, "It is not good for the man to be alone. I will make a helper who is right for him."*

*19 From the ground God formed every wild animal and every bird in the sky, and he brought them to the man so the man could name them. Whatever the man called each living thing, that became its name.*

*20 The man gave names to all the tame animals, to the birds in the sky, and to all the wild animals. But Adam, did not find a helper that was right for him.*

Here we see God sees man cannot handle his tasks alone, so he creates Eve to be a helper for him. Let's make sure we understand the definition of a helper. Dictionary.com says that a helper is a person or thing that helps or gives assistance or support. Other words for helper include: aide, helpmate, coworker, workmate, teammate, colleague, and partner.

Society has deemed a helper or a teammate as someone of lesser value, but the truth is every teammate has value. Every partner holds worth and should be someone who is truly committed to the cause and makes a clear choice to be in this thing until the end. You can't get it done without them. We all have to understand the importance of being a good teammate. For those of you who may have played sports in your early days or maybe you're in an adult recreation league now, either way, at some point, you have to have an understanding of how to learn and play your key position. None of us have what it takes to operate in every position at the same time. It takes too much energy. It's difficult for one person to have the stamina to remain productive, but we must understand each role and play our part well.

There's a saying that reminds us to "Stay in your Lane." This is a driving reference that teaches us that it is impossible for us to maintain control when we are struggling to stay in our own lane. This is where most of us get messed up. At times we think we can do it all on our own. We must understand this is the reason God gave man a helper. The truth is, man was not created for the woman, but the woman was created for the man. So fellas, let's stop walking around as if WE are "God's Gift." God knew exactly what he was doing.

The problem most of us face is that we don't know how to function as a team player when it comes to our relationships. Again, no one has ever taught us this. In sports, it seems the biggest name always collects the biggest check, but when it comes to relationships, the ultimate payoff is an equal share of an amazing relationship. No matter how good Michael Jordan, Kobe Bryant or Lebron James are, they could never have what it takes to win alone. They need the other players to step up and play their role. In order to win, they need the RIGHT people who understand the game well enough to play their own POSITION like no one else could. This is what God realized with Adam. He saw that he needed a teammate. Someone who could play their own position to reach the desired goal of the team. The first step in achieving this is knowing the goal. After years of bad decisions in my relationships, I finally realized one of my biggest issues was I never had a goal. In my mind, the ultimate goal was simply to live comfortably and peacefully. While these are great goals, they are too broad. The plans and goals for you relationship must be specific and clear. When things are made completely clear from the beginning, it eliminates the guess work. It takes away the doubt and fearful questions such as "Are we there yet?" More on that questioning in a minute.

I would like to go back for just a minute and take a look at the process Adam had to go through to get to his Eve. In Genesis 2:18, it states God decided to make him a helper, but the very next verse says that God brought the animals before Adam. Question. Why did God bring the animals to Adam instead of just creating Eve? I believe it was because God intentionally gave Adam the "Power of Choice" in order to select the mate he thought would be the best fit for him even though God had a design in mind all along. Verse 20 then says Adam named all of the animals but did not find a mate that was right for him. This tell us that Adam had the ability to choose his mate.

Here's a little sidebar: For the single women who may be reading this book, understand this. If you have to choose him something is out of order. The option of the choice was given specifically to the man. If you have been in a long term relationship and you are doing everything that married couples do but without a marriage certificate, he is out of position. If you have to ask him to marry you, maybe you're with the wrong man. If you start a race from the wrong position, it's called a false start and everyone is made to go back to their original position. The last thing you want to do is start a relationship off in the wrong position. Think of it this way, no matter how beautiful a rose may be, it's designed to care for itself until it has been picked and in the hands of the person who makes the decision to care for it. Now, from here, let's look at the next step in the process. Let's look at Genesis 2:21 (NCV).

*21 So the Lord God caused the man to sleep very deeply, and while he was asleep, God removed one of the man's ribs. Then God closed up the man's skin at the place where he took the rib. 22 The Lord God used the rib from the man to make a woman, and then he brought the woman to the man.*

I believe that this is key when it comes to our relationships. I truly believe this is where we as men get out of position. In my high school years, we used the term, "Don't sleep on me." Which meant, don't underestimate me and miss out on what I bring to the table. I believe this same "sleep" pattern is very much relevant when it comes to men and our relationships. One of three scenarios takes place based on how men "sleep" when it comes to relationships.

#1. Oversleep. This pertains to the men who take years to commit to someone. They have a never ending list of issues when it comes to their relationships as well as a never ending list of ex's or "friends." Remember the Uncle I mentioned earlier? Cool and laid back with plenty of women in his life, but alone. They come across as picky and having extremely high standards. Some may even appear as conceited. These are the men who wait until much later in life to marry and in some cases never marry and simply miss out on the woman God had designed specifically for them. They "Sleep" on them.

#2. Under Sleep. They awaken before the process is complete. They get into many relationships at an early age and haven't yet reached the full maturity required to handle a serious relationship properly. They don't like to be alone. They rarely go much time without being in some type of relationship. These are men who more than likely marry several times genuinely trying to find Mrs. Right. They pick up unnecessary baggage along the way and deal with as well as dish out a lot of hurt in the process. This was me and I believe most men.

#3. Proper Sleep. These are men who keep to themselves with no problem. They are ok when they are not in a relationship. As a matter of fact, these are the men who limit sharing their heart or any other part of themselves. They more than likely will not have a reputation of being a lady's man and probably won't have a long list of former girlfriends and they are not affected by the peer pressure young men sometimes struggle with. These are men who will make great husbands but more times than not will date much later than their counterparts because they are not pushed by a sense of urgency to cease from being alone.

These three types are essential for us to understand and recognize when it comes to our relationships. If not, we spend most of our lives searching and being disappointed due to our lack of patience through the process. Most of us don't like process. I get it. We live in a fast-paced, microwave society. We want it fast, we want it our own way and we want it now. The problem with this mentality as it pertains to relationships is that we don't allow things to get to a level of full maturity, so we end up playing a lot of childish yet expensive games that cost more than we really want to spend in the long run. Look at the results of what happens when we wait on God to point us in the right direction.

Genesis 2:23 (New Century Version)
*23 And the man said, "Now, this is someone whose bones came from my bones, whose body came from my body. I will call her*

*'woman,' because she was taken out of man."*
*24 So a man will leave his father and mother and be united with his wife, and the two will become one body.*

When we take the full advantage of the process and embrace it, the chances of us missing out on the one that God designed for us from the beginning is slim to none. Unfortunately, I believe that most of us don't actually miss out on that person, but instead, I believe in most cases, we come across that person and at times we simply mess up the opportunity by not staying in position. We either over sleep or under sleep and this creates a detour. These detours are designed to help get you to the place He designed or redesigned for you. Choosing HIS pathway from the beginning will make all the difference in the world, but you must hear and heed His voice to do so.

It is important to understand the position we hold as well as the position others hold in our life. In Genesis chapter 3, we see how things got messed up and how we've been out of position ever since.

Out Of Position - Genesis 3:1-6 (NCV)

*1 Now the snake was the most clever of all the wild animals the Lord God had made. One day the snake said to the woman, "Did God really say that you must not eat fruit from any tree in the garden?"*
*2 The woman answered the snake, "We may eat fruit from the trees in the garden.*

*3 But God told us, 'You must not eat fruit from the tree that is in the middle of the garden. You must not even touch it, or you will die.'*

*4 But the snake said to the woman, "You will not die.*

*5 God knows that if you eat the fruit from that tree, you will learn about good and evil and you will be like God!"*

*6 The woman saw that the tree was beautiful, that its fruit was good to eat, and that it would make her wise. So she took some of its fruit and ate it. She also gave some of the fruit to her husband who was with her, and he ate it.*

Now let's recap. Adam's job was to "Oversee the earth and have dominion over the animals who God gave him the task of naming. (Gen 2:15,19 NCV) The first question that comes to my mind when I read the story of Eve's deception is, Why was Adam allowing something that He named, to carry on a conversation with the woman HE chose? Why was he not walking in his authority by putting a stop to this conversation? What made him step out of position and leave his wife uncovered? Men, we must understand that a woman's number one need is security. This is why she asks you so many questions. It's the reason why she needs details. It's not that she is just being nosey or wanting to bug you for answers, she just requires answers to create the security keeps her in a good place. Having answers gives her the security that she needs. If a woman tells you she hears a noise in the car, it's your job to check it out until she no longer hears it or at least has a good explanation of what it is. Why?

Because it gives her security when driving. If she is awakened in the middle of the night to a startling sound, but yet you are sound asleep, she is going to wake you up because she needs you to get up and go check it out. Why? Because it's your job to make her feel safe. The more answers a woman has, the safer and at peace she will be. The less amount of answers she has, the less secure she will feel.

Anytime the security of a woman is threatened, her trust has the potential of being placed in the hands of someone or something else. The last thing any man should want is for the woman HE is supposed to cover to begin to feel like she has to be covered by someone other than him. Adam stepped out of position and we have been fighting to get that position back ever since.

Now ladies, don't think you're in the clear. Our fair damsel, Mrs. Eve stepped out of position as well. Not that it was her fault. Oh no, let's put that blame on Adam where it belongs. But the truth is, there was still some responsibility on Eve's part to control who she was allowing to speak into her life and relationship. Ladies, you must guard your ears when it comes to your relationships because everyone who is talking to you about your life, love and relationships isn't there to encourage you. Some people are intentionally trying to cause you to focus on the negatives so they can catch you out of position in order to take over.

Look at Eve's conversation again. She's minding her own business when the snake steps up to her and begins to talk to her about what was going on in her life. Pay attention to how the snake approached her. He came with questions. Remember what I said about women asking questions and seeking answers for security? The snake was smart enough to know he could get into her mind and get her to come up with some answers. Ladies, be careful of people who approach you with a lot of questions about your relationship. You may be entertaining a snake. These were just a few of the lessons I had to learn. I had to recognize I was out of position and acknowledge the damage I had created and allowed to take place. I had to be real with myself and address these issues not as a simple bible story, but as life lessons that would later shape the man I have now become. I wondered why I continually found myself in crazy positions in my life. It was because I simply failed to understand that blessings come to a position, not a person. The people who are in the position God intended them to be in will receive every blessing designed for that position. Unfortunately, most of us mistake our desire to be in a specific position as God's will for our lives. For many years, I was unsure of the will of God for my life, so I simply lived my life attempting to walk in the gifts God gave me. I thought because I could sing, preach and teach that these things were my "God-Ordained" purpose and position. I tried to sing like my favorite artists because I thought I was better at imitating them than I was at simply being myself. When Fred Hammond or John P. Kee came out with an awesome praise and worship track, I was all over it. I'm sure the praise team and choir I was over at the time were getting sick of me and my musical selections for worship. I was so busy trying to be them that I didn't know how to be Eric.

For years I allowed the people around me to dictate my choices. If the people wanted me to sing, I did it, even when I wasn't really feeling it. I allowed people to determine what Eric was good at and continued to stay in that area even when I knew God was calling me to something different; something higher. I let the opinions of others tell me my gifting to sing was greater than my calling to truly minister the word of God. See, I'm a church boy at heart. Born and raised. I

> You will be much happier when you get delivered from the opinions from other people.

knew exactly what to do, what to sing and how to sing it to stir up the people emotionally, but the whole time, I was seeing it as a spiritual thing. Trust me, with the stuff that was weighing on me at the time, there was nothing spiritual about it. It was all flesh.

The truth is, my gifts were given to me as functions instead of positions. They were merely the vehicles and tools God gave me in order to be able to walk in my true anointed original design and position. Because I did not know my true purpose for so many years, I found myself stuck in places that no longer felt good. I remember, at one point I could hide behind the music. It was a persona that kept hidden the pain, the struggles and the insecurities of an overweight preacher's kid who didn't really like who he was. I simply became an adult overweight preacher who didn't like who he was. I was no longer fulfilled by singing. It simply became "That thing" I used to do but no longer sought refuge in it. You've got to make the decision to come to this point in your own life. You will be happier when you get delivered from the opinions from other people. Stop seeking other people's approval to move into God's calling for your life. You will be more fulfilled. Until you find the strength to do this, you will find yourself in a place of frustration and disappointment. Through it all, remember, "Failure is only failure when you fail to learn from it."

## KEYS TO REMEMBER:

- Protect your relationships by guarding your conversation
- Blessings are designed for a position, not a person
- Get delivered from the opinions of other people

*Interested in booking Eric for speaking engagements, marriage conferences, retreats or singles events?*
*Go to www.realtalkconsultants.com today.*

## 5 A FRESH START

With all of the transitions that had occurred in my life at this point, it was time to begin again. I don't know about you but I have always found starting over to be one of the most difficult things for me. Getting back to basics is difficult when you've never learned them. I learned that my successes give me drive and my failures cause me to stop. I now understood, like every other man, my number one need was success. I also learned I could not depend on anyone else to provide this success for me. It was all on me. It was not that I had to bring home the biggest paycheck or drive the best car, but it was so much deeper than that. I realized what I thought and said about myself would make the greatest difference.

I had to begin to see myself as a success and not a failure. Again, failing does not make you a failure. You must learn from your mistakes. What worked? What didn't? What could you have done better? It was all about my perspective.

So there I was. Twice divorced, still unsure of my purpose, although I knew it was not simply to entertain others with my ability to sing. At this time, a couple of years had passed. I was searching for a new church home, a new job and possibly someone new in my life. I decided it was time for me to actually get out and do something I honestly had absolutely no experience in. Dating. I had no desire to just meet someone and get immediately back into a relationship.

I'd to do something different if I wanted to see a different result. I went into it with the mindset that I was searching for a friend and companion, not a girlfriend. To be honest, the term "Girlfriend" didn't even sound the same at 32 years old. The girl that my former roommate was dating was begging me to meet her friend so that maybe we could hang out together as a group. After some time, I finally gave in. I was in my own place at this time and I decided to have everyone over to my place for drinks and game night. My friend got there late, but I was prepared for that. I had given him an earlier time because I knew he wouldn't show up on time. I wanted him there before the ladies got there. A little later, there was a knock at the door. I nervously opened the door to see his girlfriend and one of the prettiest women I had come across in a while standing there. I quickly invited them in, took their coats and ushered them to their seats.

We had a blast that night. No pressure. No one expecting anything other than to have a good time. It was the best time I had had in a long time. It was a good feeling. We ended the night pretty late and I walked my new friend to her car. My nerves were shot. Although we had just had an amazing time, I was at a loss. I didn't know what to do next. Remember, this was all new to me. It had been a long time. We stood at her car and talked for another hour, she got in her car and we exchanged phone numbers and planned our next get together. We talked on the phone for a few days and finally decided on our first official date. In our conversations, we explained our circumstances to one another. Not too much detail but just enough to begin getting to know each other.

We discussed how we both had kids from previous relationships and how we wanted to make sure we did not allow our new friendship to impact them in anyway. This meant the kids would not know about us. We both felt like this was the best idea seeing that we were getting to know each other ourselves. It was way too soon for all of that. I get to her house that night and before I could get out of the car to knock on the door, one of the cutest little girls came flying out of the house. She was about nine years old and running full speed to my car. Her pig tails bouncing in the wind and a big smile on her face. She ran straight to my back door, opened it and jumped in. As I turned around she said "Hi, You must be my mommy's friend, Eric. Where are ya'll going? Can I go?" I was stunned. Are you kidding me? This was exactly what we had been talking about. As I sat there in shock, I turned to see her mom walking towards the car with another child. This time, it was her 15 year old. They get to the car and she looks in the passenger window and says, "Do you mind if we drop them off at my mom's house?" Immediately, I'm thinking to myself. Wait, so not only am I meeting both of your kids on our first date, but now I've got to go to your mom's house? This was unreal. I didn't know what to say. I said, "Sure." She introduces me to the girls and we were off. The whole ride to her mother's house, I am still at a loss for words. I'm cordial, but shocked and kind of pissed off.

I began to notice that every time I looked in my rear view mirror, the girls were looking at me and grinning. Oh God! What have I gotten myself into? We pull up to her mom's house and the girls jump out. They were very polite kids. They turned back to me and said thank you with those same smiles on their little faces and then ran to their grandmother's porch. She takes the girls in as I'm sitting in the car waiting. Within a few minutes, I see the door open and I'm thinking, great! We can finally get this date started. I see someone waving their arms around, so I turn towards the door. Guess who? You guessed it...MOM! She's standing on the porch waving trying to get my attention. I reluctantly roll down my window and she says, "Hey, you must be Eric! Well, come on in so I can meet you!" You gotta be kidding me! This cannot be happening to me right now! I already had to meet your kids and now I'm being forced to come and meet your mom, ON OUR FIRST DATE? Who does this?

I get out of the car, walk up to the porch and I hear mom scream, "It's open! Come on in!" I walk in and the first person I see is my date. She is looking at me like she could die. I could see the apology written all over her face. Luckily, mom didn't require that we stay long. She just wanted to meet me face to face. The way the girls and the grandmother were smiling, you would think we were going to the prom or something. Anyway, we quickly returned to the car. Once we reached the car, she leaned over and grabbed my hand and began to apologize as if her life depended on it. Little did she know, it did. I smiled and accepted her apology and we move on with the date. We had planned to catch dinner and a movie. We choose the movie first. We had a ball. Amazing time just watching the movie and getting to know more about one another.

As we were heading to the restaurant, my phone

rings. It's my daughter, Alexis. Remember, this is my baby. She was a daddy's girl having a daddy moment and needed me. She was having a hard time dealing with her mom and I splitting up. Each time I got this call, it tore me apart. I hated she felt this way, but I knew that it was a mourning process and would take time. I turned to my date and apologized. I told her I needed to go check on her and that it would only take a few minutes. I offered to take her back to her house since it was not too far from my daughter and when I was done, I would come back to get her to finish our date. I was not ready for what came next.

She looked at me with pure shock in her eyes. She couldn't understand why I wanted to "pause" my date with her to go and check on my daughter. She wanted to know why she couldn't just go with me. Uhh..How about...NO! We've talked about this for two weeks and I just met half of your family! I explained that my kids were not ready to see me with anyone else. They were still struggling with me not being with their mother. I was not about to let them see me with someone else this soon. She just couldn't seem to understand this and ultimately advised me of her disagreement with my choice. I was done. I knew this would not go any further. If she couldn't respect my choices regarding my kids, she more than likely wouldn't appreciate my opinions on her own. I drove straight to her house to drop her off. I had more important things to do. We pulled up at her house. I thanked her for a cool night out and told her to have a good one. She looked at me in shock, got out to my car and got into her own. I guess she was headed back to her mom's house to tell them how the date went. This experience taught me a few of things.

**Number One:** Dating had changed as I knew it. Seeing that I had been in relationships at a young age and married for the first time by the age of 17, I had no real experience in dating. For the first time, I was put in the position to find out what it was truly like. I had no clue what I was in for. Maybe I didn't know what to expect. Maybe I was expecting too much.

**Number Two:** She was out of her mind! The very thing we talked about the most was the protection of our kids. We didn't want to expose them to people too soon, yet she almost takes them on our first date! Bad move.

**Number Three:** Anyone who expected me to choose them over my children did not have my children's best interest at heart and obviously did not know me well at all. I was a lot of things, but an absent, irresponsible father was not in my description.

Through it all, I came to the realization that I had to change the way I thought dating was supposed to go. I had to gather a plan on how I wanted to do this, but most importantly, I had to get a clear understanding of my own expectations and clearly relay this to the other person. Whenever you sit across from someone you are considering, be sure that you are looking at the person they are and not the person you wished they were.

> **Be sure that you are looking at the person they are and not the person you wish they were.**

Remember, dating is a consideration of truth about the man/woman you intend to spend the rest of your life with; don't lie to yourself to make somebody be something they are not. Remember, dating is an interview, not an obligation! I got really serious about not making the same mistakes again. I set some ground rules for myself. It later became what I now call my **5 RealTalk Tips for Dating**.

**1. There is NO biblical reference on dating.** This is simply because marriages were arranged. With that being said, the only thing you can pull from scripture as it concerns dating is how to treat people in general. The Song of Solomon speaks on intimacy and several other scriptures make reference to sex, but you will find none on dating. Our western mindsets find it hard to grasp the process of an arranged relationship.

In most Eastern cultures, the parents choose their children's mates. Many from birth. Most of us cannot even begin to fathom our parent's picking out our mates for us, but ask yourself this question: If you and someone of the opposite sex have been trained since birth on what the other person's likes, dislikes and habits, what are the chances of that marriage having longevity that most of our first marriages do not? If you still think this is a crazy tactic, just think of it this way, what kinds of choices have YOU made on your own? Just a thought.

**2. Stop dating with such high expectations.** So much emphasis is placed on building a relationship that we fail to focus on building a friendship. Loving someone is amazing but liking them will make the difference. Most people meet someone and after a few conversations and dates, they have laid claim to that person as if they are exclusive already. I believe the mindsets have to change when it comes to dating. This should be the time that you are just getting to know the person and allowing them to get to know you. We become too serious way too soon. If you go out with someone one day and see them out with someone else the next, you have no right to get all emotional and hurt because they are with someone else. This is too soon for these types of strong emotions. You have got to learn to control this in a more productive way.

Dating is simply an opportunity for you to collect data on a person. The problem is that most people go into dating with either very high expectations or absolutely no expectations at all. High expectations will lead to disappointment while no expectations can leave you overwhelmed. Take your time and meet people and enjoy the time and companionship without your emotions getting in the way. Let a friendship develop before you allow emotions to come in to play. As you take more time to get to know someone, you may begin to see that it's just not a good fit for either you or them. You can only figure this out by investing emotion free time before going all in.

**3. The meeting of the representatives.** When we first meet someone, we all do our best to impress the person. We want to come across as together emotionally, financially, physically, mentally and socially. We don't want to show any flaws but if we do, we want them to be as small as possible to appear somewhat "normal." Some people can suppress who they really are for only a short period of time, but most of the time we don't find out the truth until a couple of months down the line when we have a disagreement.

This is when the real person comes to the surface. A selfish person will not appear this way in the beginning. They will come across as the most giving person in the world, but they will not be able to maintain this for long, simply because it is not who they truly are at heart. If a person has control issues, this may not be apparent within the first few months, but as soon as that person feels the need to point the relationship in the direction they want it to go, that sweet, gentle person is out the window and is not likely to return.

## WHAT TO DO ABOUT IT?

**4. Time and Focus is of the essence.** I heard this saying a lot when I was younger. I always assumed that it was mainly saying time was short so use it wisely. While this may be true, I believe it also means that time is the soul or the nature of a positive outcome. Only through time can we see what a child will grow up to be. Through time we have the ability to learn something we did not know when it came to our past experiences. My son, EJ, is an artist. When he was a little boy, he began to scribble on whatever he could get his hands on. Usually it was my walls instead of some blank paper.

One day while I was admiring the artwork of my two year old on my bedroom walls, I began to recognize the doddles he blessed us with. I started to notice the shapes of the characters. All of a sudden I could see who they were. I told his mom, "That's Mike Wizowski from Monster's Inc!" She laughed at me and said that I had been watching too many of the kids movies. I called him into the room and said, "EJ, who is that?" He began to chant the mantra I had taught him during his punishments. "We write on paper not on walls!" As I laughed, I pulled him close to me and let him know he wasn't in trouble. "Daddy just wants to know who the characters are." I said. He slowly began to go around the room and tell me the identity of each little character he had previously drawn. "That's Sully from Monster's Inc. and that's Sebastian from Little Mermaid." I could see it! They were no longer doddles! They were art! So what made them change from doddles to artwork? It wasn't like he had updated them with color or extra doodles. It was that I finally took the "Time" to "Focus" and then I could see what they truly were. These two things are essential when it comes to relationships, but it must start from the beginning. If we pay attention from the start and if we don't allow our emotions to take over, we can begin to see what really lies beneath the surface.

**5. Levels of attraction.** I really began to look at what I was attracted too. There's an old saying that says

"Opposites attract." While this may be true in some cases, I honestly believe in other cases, we attract what we are. Whether it's someone on our same level in one way or another, ultimately, there is something about you that attracts the type of people that you do. This is an area we must take special time and care to recognize. I look at dating as having 5 different levels of attraction. This is what attracts or draws us to another person. We need to be careful with these. If we base everything about the relationship on these or use this information in the wrong way, the attraction will be all we have. When that fades, we are left with a shell of what might have been a really good relationship but we ruined it by our focus on superficial, surface type concerns.

• **Physical** – This is common in both men and women. Some might say that men struggle with this more than women, but being a man and seeing this with my female friends, I believe this an equal struggle between the sexes. We all have personal preferences when it comes to what we like and don't like in a person. Tall, short, heavy, skinny, dark, light, good teeth, great skin. It's all surface stuff and ultimately should have no bearing on the type of person we are. We can't get stuck here. I had an uncle told me and my brothers to stop looking at the little hot, girls. He said we had better start looking at their moms. As I got older, I understood what he meant. Our genes play a major part in how we look, act and think. This was good information to know, but it should not be the foundation of the relationship.

• **Mental** – Do you match on an intellectual level? Are you able to hold a good conversation about more than just the weather, kids, family and activities? You must be able to connect with someone on a level deeper than their looks and likes alone. You need to understand how they think. How they process things.

How they handle stress. This can also help you to recognize if there may be some control issues. As you find out information about a person's family and friends, it is very important to see how they handle those relationships. Ladies: What's the relationship like between him and his mother or sisters? What about a father type connection? If you look at his role models, do you see or hear the characteristics you are looking for in a mate. Gentlemen: What is her relationship with her father or some other male role model? How does she get along with her mother, sisters or friends? All of these things are key elements that will ultimately impact you if you are considering spending more time with them.

• **Emotional** – Are they emotionally secure? Can you make a heart connection? Most people get involved with people based merely on what a person looks like or what a person can do for them. Both of these have the potential to change. You must get to know someone on a deeper level. Now, I know this may be a difficult issue especially for the ladies because most men do not share their emotions. The truth is, most men have never been taught how to process their own emotions. Most of our lives, men have been told to suck it up, hold it in, take it like a man. Well, allow me to kill a myth right here. Real men are emotionally responsible. Meaning we can recognize where we are and handle things accordingly by compartmentalizing what's important and what's unnecessary.

Now ladies, don't think this is all about the men, because you have some emotional responsibilities as well. Women have to be careful not to be overly emotional, especially in the very beginning. You have to understand that if you pour out all of your emotions at one time on a man who has never been taught to handle his own emotions, you will overwhelm him and more than likely drive him away. You have the same responsibility to prioritize and compartmentalize your emotions in order to express them at the right times and with the right strength.

• **Spiritual** – This can be a touchy area. The balance of a relationship can hinge on this one attraction alone. There are some who think that because a person attends a church service on a regular basis, that this makes them a spiritual person. This is not true. The truth is, there are those who go to church merely to find someone who they view as spiritual in order to gain a relationship. Let's get an understanding of exactly what this means. Spirituality is the practical demonstration of positive characteristics that are expressed throughout ones daily life.

When meeting someone for the first time, don't get trapped because they attend services regularly. Take the time to be sure they have the same moral mindset, convictions, desires, values and attitudes towards life that you do. If you are willing to bend too much in this area, you could pay more than you are willing to pay all because you are trying to yoke yourself with someone who may not have the intentions of going in the same direction you may be headed. Being "Unequally Yoked" does not pertain only to the spiritual, but to the natural as well. You are unequally yoked with anyone whose goals, dreams, intentions and practices go in a different direction than yours. Don't settle for simply being on the same page as someone else, but make sure you're coming from the same book.

REALTALK: The Making of a Man

# 6 MY EXPECTATIONS

Growing up in a home where my brother's and I literally never heard my parents fight or argue was an amazing experience we honestly took for granted until we got older. We couldn't really appreciate how they shielded us as kids but we also never realized how damaging it would be when it came to our own marriages.

My brothers and I all went into marriage expecting to have the same type of relationship our parents had. No drama, no fighting and no arguing, especially in front of the kids. Though these were great expectations to have, they were not realistic. We failed to think about the fact that the women we married were not raised in the same home we were. We had never seen conflict in the home so we were not used to it. Not only that, but we also never learned how to resolve conflict. These were our expectations, but they were not the expectations of our wives. To be perfectly honest with you, I wonder if my brothers even knew what their wives expected in their marriage. Personally, I never asked about her expectations. It wasn't even discussed. Here's another truth I've learned. "Your expectations are based on your experiences." How do we go into a relationship expecting our mate to understand what we expect yet we've never had a conversation about it? It's impossible. It doesn't matter how long you have known each other. If you never take time to discuss what you are looking for in a relationship, there is no possible way for them to know. This was so unfair on my part. To go into a marriage without ever discussing what we thought, dreamed or wanted in our relationship was just wrong. We were setting ourselves up for disaster from the beginning.

The truth is, we teach people how to love us. How can you expect someone else to know something that you never tell them? Well, this is how we went into our marriages.

A couple of years ago, I did a study on the top 10 reasons that marriages fail. After looking at all of the data that I found, here is what I came up with:

#10 Time
#9 Expectations
#8 Personality
#7 Abuse

#6 Addiction
#5 Friends
#4 Sex
#3 Family
#2 Communication
#1 Finances

It hurts me to say that every single one of these issues plagued my marriages on one level or another. Notice that Communication (#2) and Expectations (#9) are both on the list, but I have come to the conclusion that these two, more than any of the other topics have an impact on the reason for every divorce. It's not simply the issues on the list, but it's the communication and expectations of each area that play the biggest roles. In other words, it's not simply time, but the fact that people are getting married without communicating their expectations as it pertains to their time. For example; most never discuss how much time their spouse requires of them.

Work, home and extracurricular activities all have a place in our daily lives, but we don't discuss how we will handle these concerns prior to it being an issue. It's not just the personality traits, but it's the fact that we don't discuss our expectations about someone's personality. Often, when we have gotten to the point where we are thinking of marriage, we have looked beyond our mate's personality issues to the point where we either accept it as being who they are or we tolerate it and secretly want to change them. Even when it comes to sex, it's rarely the sex itself, but it's the frequency and quality of sex we have failed to address prior to getting deeply involved in the relationship. We spend so much time chasing the one who we think is the "Right" person that we fail to check to be sure they are the right person for US.

This explains why I had so many issues in my past relationships when it came to communication an expectations. These were the types of deep, detailed conversations we failed to have with one another. How in the world did we expect someone else to read our minds and just know what it is we were missing? It was impossible. It all comes back to each person clearly communicating what they expected in the marriage.

In marriage, we normally focus on two sets of expectations. The husband's and the wife's, but the truth is, there are three sets: What the husband expects, what the wife expects and what the marriage expects. We fail to discuss the first two most of the time because most people tend to assume that their mate, along with everyone else, should think just like they do. The truth is, no one has ever taught us about the expectations of the marriage, but there are some fundamental elements God has placed within the institution of marriage itself that must be addressed along with each spouse's personal requirements. Here are a few marital expectations.

A relationship with another person will NEVER complete you. The goal should be for us to become whole prior to bringing someone else into our lives. Unfortunately, most of us don't know what it means to be whole. Nothing missing, nothing broken. If you are not whole before they show up, their presence won't make you whole. Understand, if you are single and attempting to find your mate, someone who is whole will NEVER search for someone who is broken. Here are a few signs to know if you're whole or not. If you're still holding onto grudges and pains from a previous relationship, you're not whole. If you still get upset when someone mentions your ex's name or brings up an old situation, you're not whole. If you go into a new relationship thinking it will heal you from the last one, you're not whole. If you think every person that you come into contact with is going to be exactly like the last one, you're not whole. If you don't see yourself as deserving of someone who will treat you the way God intended for you to be treated, you're not whole. This is an unfair situation to put the next person in. You appear whole and well put together, but underneath all the makeup and masks, you are broken and expecting them to help you carry your baggage.

**Becoming One.** Genesis 2:24 speaks of a husband and wife becoming one flesh. This does not mean they will become the same person in the natural realm, but it does mean they should be one in the spiritual realm. When people see one, they should see the other. People should recognize them as ONE entity. Couples who fail to achieve oneness will seem to be married but living single. This is dangerous, because the longer a married person operates as if they are single, the more the traits they adhered to when they were single will begin to permeate their world. Soon, you will merely be roommates. Trust me, this is not a good place to be.

**Leave and Cleave.** This is a biblical principle found in Genesis 2:24. It simply means to remove yourself from what's familiar and connect with your mate on a different level. After marriage, your mate should become your number one priority. Not kids, parents or even ministry. The order of your priorities should be God (Meaning your personal relationship), Family (Spouse being first, then children). Everything else should follow after this. As a preacher's kid, I've seen the pastor's family suffer because he was focused more on the ministry/church than his family. This is out of order. His family IS his FIRST ministry. If a man can't manage his family well, he will not be able to manage the church properly.

**What you don't understand, you must respect.** At times when we fail to understand a person's point of view, we tend to dismiss it or disrespect it all because we don't see it from the same perspective. Two different people will more than likely see the same situation two different ways. The only way to combat this is by having the ability to compromise. This cannot be achieved if either party dismisses how the other person feels. Whatever you don't respect, you will eventually abuse.

If you don't know how it's designed, you will use it in dysfunction. We must have a true understanding about how relationships should function in order for them to operate in the way they were designed. Have you ever seen someone try to use a folding chair as a ladder? How did that turn out? There are times when you can accomplish your goal that way, but eventually, all it will take is one misstep to change into a disaster. This is what we do in relationships. We assume that because we have seen it done that we can repeat what we saw. The truth is, without having the right principles in place, we are setting ourselves up to fail.

My current car is a 2014 Maxima. It's my first car

with a push button ignition. The day we bought the car, my daughter, Eboni, came home from Knoxville. We couldn't wait to show her the car. We walked outside and I went to the driver's side and I just stuck my right leg inside to push the brake. I then pushed the button to start the car and nothing happened. I did it again. Still nothing. Now, it had only been a few hours since we bought the car, so you can imagine how upset I was becoming at the thought of my new car was not starting. When I went to attempt it a third time, I noticed the digital screen on the dash that said, "No key found inside." Now I knew I had to have the key on me, but the car was unable to recognize that I had it because I was only halfway in the car. I felt like an idiot. Immediately, God spoke to me. He said, "It's just like marriage. You have got to be ALL IN for it to function properly." I realized it wasn't the car that had the problem, it was me! I wasn't working the principles the way the car was designed but I was still expecting it to function the way it was supposed to work.

This is how most people function in relationships. We have no clear understanding how they are designed to function, yet we operate in them the same way we always have and then get upset at the other person and ultimately the relationship and say it didn't work or it failed. Not true…WE failed.

The truth is, there is no set institution that enables

us to learn how to operate in relationships. Our schools, universities and our churches are not equipped to prepare us properly. Where are people supposed to get this type of information? Children are unable to learn it from parents if the parents are not aware of the principles themselves. It is imperative that we use these principles in the proper way in order to achieve the most from our relationships and marriages.

## KEYS TO REMEMBER:

- Your expectations are based on your experiences
- Honest communication is essential in a healthy relationship
- Relationships require you to be fully invested

*Interested in booking Eric for speaking engagements, marriage conferences, retreats or singles events?*
*Go to www.realtalkconsultants.com today.*

# 7 THE POTTER'S WHEEL

With all of the things I had experienced in my life, there were some key lessons I took away from it all. I learned I was not in control of anything but my own responses to the things that happened. I could not control those around me. I could not control how they behaved or even how they treated me, but what I could control was how I responded to it. I knew God had truly been working on me.

My responses to negative situations were changing. Believe me, I was nowhere near perfect and that's something I still have not attained, but what I did realize was, I was becoming a different person. I was starting to allow the change God wanted for me to manifest itself in my own life. Recently, I had an amazing conversation with a good friend of mine by the name of T. C. Whiteside. T.C. and I have not known each other for years and years like most of the people in my inner circle, but from the time we met, I knew that he was one of those people in my life. He quickly became another brother to me. He stated something during our conversation that day which ignited something in me. He mentioned the fact that most people continue to struggle through life simply because we fail to learn to live out our life on the potter's wheel. "We come down on our own too soon, because we think that we are ready to be used for the purpose for which we were specifically designed," he said. I was amazed at the illustration.

As the conversation continued, I began to see the vision of an incomplete piece of pottery removing itself from the grips of the potter's hands in an attempt to operate in the capacity that it believed it was designed. It was at this moment that I was reminded of the illustration that God gave me about the sleeping man that I spoke of in chapter four. There are those of us who are so intent on being in a relationship that we get ahead of what's intended for us and instead we create scenarios that cause more harm than good. Let's get back to my piece of pottery. If it is removed from the wheel too soon, there will be some areas that are still in need of molding.

After a little research, I found it interesting that the process of making pottery is sometimes called "Throwing a Pot." In this technique, the potter's hands are the tools. Each hand is designed for a specific task. The right hand pushes down while the left hand pushes forward. The right hand touches only half of the top surface from center to edge, while the left hand smooths the outer edge of clay with the palm. This is to not only secure the pot to the wheel, but it's a technique used to create the shape the potter sees in this pot's future. There is constant pressure and pulling throughout the process. I am sure that if the pot had feelings, this would cause some pains, but ultimately, they're growing pains. The potter may see the need to take some clay away so he removes unnecessary clay from the desired areas. Because the desired outcome of the pot is to enable it to hold something, the potter begins to pull and squeeze on the clay in order to build the wall that will eventually hold whatever the potter decides to place inside of it. All while this is going on, there is a constant spinning and a constant bathing taking place. (The water to assist in the shaping and keeping down friction. The spinning to allow the potter to keep his hands centrally located while the form is taking place.)

Through this illustration, I began to see how dangerous coming off of the potter's wheel too soon can be. This is what I believe most of us do when it comes to our relationships. We are in such a hurry that we think we're ready when the truth is, we have no idea what we are getting ourselves into. We are unprepared for the tasks and responsibilities a relationship requires.

We have not allowed the things that need to be taken away from us to be removed. Selfishness, a closed mind, an unwillingness to compromise, an attitude that it's all about you. These are the things I personally failed to rid myself of all because I did not allow the potter to complete his work before attempting to operate in something I had no experience in.

Marriage is not a happily ever after. It's not a fairytale or a picture perfect entity. It takes real effort to focus on your spouse having no real guarantee that they will return the gesture. Marriage is about each spouse meeting the needs of their mate. It's about not throwing it away when it needs a simple repair. It's about investing more in the marriage than you do the wedding. When a person goes into marriage without any idea on how to fulfill their responsibility as a spouse, it is the beginning of a long fall down a steep slope. These are some of the things I eventually figured out. Unfortunately, I spent a lot of years hurting myself and others by my decisions and actions. My number one piece of advice for anyone who is contemplating a relationship is to take serious time to evaluate yourself. Examine your reasons for wanting the relationship. Know what it takes to maintain it. Most of us struggle in relationships because we don't know how they were designed to function. Remember, when you don't understand the original design, you will use it in dysfunction. Don't get me wrong, there are those who struggle and stay in relationship for years, but those are people who have at least taken on the mindset they are going to work to make it work.

To my readers, here's some advice for you. Stay on the potter's wheel. Allow yourself to learn from every experience, but don't attempt to experience things before you are ready. You expectations are based on your experiences. The more negative the experience, the more negative the expectation. Stay on the wheel. Allow God to cut away the things you don't need. Let him prune

> Stay on the potter's wheel until your design is clear.

unforgiveness and bitterness. He needs to cut away selfishness and replace it with selflessness. When we allow God to make these changes in our lives, it not only make our relationships better but it improves our lives as well. Stay on the potter's wheel. Don't be moved by your emotions. They were not designed to move you. You were design to control them.

The potter's wheel is a place of preparation. It's a place of foundation, creation and manifestation. Stay there until HE makes it clear to you exactly what your purpose is. Find out what it is that HE has designed you to carry. Understand that what HE has allowed in your life is not just for you, but it's to impact those who you come into contact with who need your guidance and direction to manage that same circumstance in their own life. Stay on the wheel. Use your time on the wheel to be properly trained for yourself. Don't rush into the next relationship. Take your time. Think of it this way, you want to be in a position to properly teach the next person how to love you. Only you can do that. But if you have no idea how to love you, it will be impossible for you to teach someone else. Let the master finish his work before you begin adding accessories that might not fit, properly. Stay on the potter's wheel. Someone else needed to hear this one, T.C. Thanks for sharing that word! Love you, Man!

*Interested in booking Eric for speaking engagements, marriage conferences, retreats or singles events?*
*Go to www.realtalkconsultants.com today.*

## 8 FINDING SUCCESS

After a few years of seriously trying to work on me, I felt the need to begin finding that one person God had just for me. Not simply to cure the lonely feeling that stepped in from time to time, but to find that helpmate HE desired for me. To be honest with you, I didn't like being alone. It was difficult.

Over the years, although my relationships were trying and sometimes volatile, I missed being with someone. I believe this feeling is what causes most people to get into unhealthy relationships they can't seem to get out. They find comfort in simply being with someone. It's amazing how we can become so conditioned to just being with someone that we will tolerate the dysfunction even after we realize they are not the right person for us. I didn't want to make the same mistakes. Not just the things I felt were done to me, but I didn't want to go into my next relationship as the same man I had been in the previous ones. I had to be different. The next one would be for keeps. The next one would be forever. The next one would push me into my purpose.

Throughout my struggles in relationships, I learned there are two things that build successful patterns in marriage. A man must have the ability to properly communicate and strengthen his wife emotionally and a woman must be able to encourage and celebrate her husband more than she casts blame. You can only achieve a happy marriage when the two people involved understand these two principles and when the reasons for getting married are greater than the stressors that come along with marriage.

In Genesis 3, it wasn't simply the fall of man, but the fall of marriage. I had to go into it with the understanding that the natural order of things may not always be God's order. I had to understand the enemy is always working against marriage because it is an institution ordained by God, but we must also understand there is always something greater in the spirit realm that's working for you. This is what ties marriage together. It's the final strand in the tri-cord equation. Ecclesiastes 4:12 (NCV) says "An enemy might defeat one person, but two people together can defend themselves; but a rope that is woven of three strings is hard to break." There will always be struggles, but without God as a source of foundation and common ground, these struggles will seem insurmountable. What is the glue that will bind you together?

I wanted something different. I sought God and chose not to follow my flesh. There were times when my flesh got weak and I wanted to go after what caught my eye instead of my spirit, but I kept reminding myself of my past decisions. I had to do something I had never done to become something I had never been. I had to go places I had never been in order to see something I had never seen. I refused to repeat my past. I wanted what God had for me more than ever. There's a saying that goes: "People come into our lives for a reason, a season or a lifetime." I've learned we must use the discernment God gave us in order to place people in the correct category. One of the biggest mistakes we can make is placing "Seasonal" people in "Lifetime" positions. By doing this, we basically set them up for failure due to no fault of their own. Sometimes there are people directly in front of us who God has placed there for "Lifetime" positions that we overlook because what we see in them does not match up to our list of wants, needs or desires. I wanted to be sure I was not guilty of missing the blessing God has designed for me due to shallow desires.

There was a woman whom I had known for years. We grew up in the same church as kids and I had watched her battle her own struggles in marriage. Over the years, Deborah and I had become really good friends. As a matter of fact, she had become my best friend. She began singing in my gospel group and she worked closely with me keeping the calendar and books for the ministry. I could tell her anything without fear of being judged. I could trust her enough to know what I told her would not go any further. That was something I thought I had in the past, but later learned that was not the case. Because of our friendship, we always talked about our issues and we celebrated our successes. It was a friendship I had never really experienced with anyone before.

A couple of years after my divorce, she went through her own. Like always, we were there to help each other through the rough patches in our lives. After having lunch with her one day, I began to see her a little differently. I couldn't explain it. It was like I was that shy, scared teenager again. I wasn't really sure what I was feeling, and I definitely wasn't about to tell her. Afraid of flat out rejection, I kept my thoughts and feelings to myself. A few months went by and the feelings began to get stronger. I couldn't understand what it was. There was a part of me that liked the feeling yet another part of me was scared to death. I reached out to another friend of mine. I began to tell her how I was feeling and how afraid I was. Johnika took the time to listen and minister to me. She never gave any directions as far as how to approach Deborah, but just encouraged me to keep pursing and to follow my heart.

After about a year, there was a boldness that crept up within me. My feelings were growing daily and I was about to explode not telling her how I was feeling. I finally made the decision to tell her. It went nothing like I was expecting. She was having the same feelings and thoughts that I was. WHEW!! What a relief! My fear was gone. No longer was I concerned with the thoughts of rejection I allowed to plague my mind in the past. Although I still had doubts about myself, it was just my desire to be sure I was making the right decisions and I was ready. Could I be the man for her I wasn't for the others? Had I grown enough to overcome the selfishness I had grown to tolerate in my life? These were questions I asked myself every day. I didn't want to repeat my past. I wanted to be a better person, a better man and a better husband.

Deborah and I sat down and discussed a lot of things over the next two years. We knew we didn't want to repeat our past, so we talked about our "non-negotiables." These were the things we were determined not to budge on. They were standards that would cause us to walk away if we were unable to agree in these areas. I kept thinking back to what my dad told me years before this. "We just made a decision." Deb and I made several decisions. The biggest one being, this was it. If we were going to make this work, we had to focus on the needs of the other and the "D" word was COMPLETELY off the table.

We decided that if it got difficult, we would seek help. We wanted this to work. After two years of dating exclusively, we decided to make it official and announce our engagement. Our friends were ecstatic! Some of our family had their own issues with it, but it wasn't about them. This was our decision. I was focused on her and she was focused on me. No one else could come between us. Anyone who tried would soon learn that we meant what we said about becoming ONE FLESH.

On August 25th, 2007, my life changed forever. I truly found the favor of God was spoken of in Proverbs 18:22 (NCV). "A man who finds a wife, finds a good thing and obtains favor from the Lord." There is a real significance to our wedding date as well as the number of this chapter. After we got married, I was home one day, just playing around with numbers on a scratch sheet of paper. I wrote down Deb's birthdate, August 17th. (8th month/ 1+7=8) Our Anniversary, August 25th. (8th month) and My birthdate, September 2nd. (9th month) As I looked at this equation, I realized that the timeframe between Deb's birthday, our anniversary and my birthday was exactly eight days.

I went to look up the meaning of the number eight. "New Beginning." The number nine means "Divine Completeness." Like never before, I could see God was placing us in the positions HE had designed for us all along.

All this time, I never truly understood what a good thing marriage could be. I had seen my parents operate in an amazing marriage, but I had no guideline or blueprint showing me how to do it. Immediately, Deb and I began to share with others how happy we truly were. It was amazing to see the smiles on people's faces when we walked into a room. Although I knew her immediate family for years, the time came for me to meet the rest of the clan. We were invited to her Cousin, Jackie's house for a Christmas dinner. I assumed it would be a handful of people. Jackie and her husband, Lin, their cousin Ginger and maybe a few others. We pulled up and couldn't find a place to park. I wanted to pass out. We walked in and everyone is staring at us. I could hear their thoughts. "Who is this joker?" Everyone was sweet and cordial.

We walked into the living room, took off our coats and my beautiful wife clears her throat and makes an announcement. "Ahem...Excuse me everyone!! I want to let you know that I am remarried and this is my new husband, Eric!" I wanted to faint. Everyone screamed, "HEY ERIC!" and then began to shake my hand and introduce themselves. It was great. We walked into the kitchen. There I met her cousin, Gerri. She was as tall as I was and she was staring at me like I was from another planet until she finally spoke. "Honey, I don't know you from a can of paint, but whatever you're doing to make my little cousin smile like that, keep it up. I haven't seen her smile like this in years." I could breathe again. Her cousin Jackie later explained that with all of the things Deb had experienced in her past, she had begun to "wear her misery." But now she was wearing her joy. I was proud. I knew I had never had that type of effect on the women in my past. At least not long term. For the past seven years, although we've had our rough patches, we never allowed the rough patches to have us. It was a decision we made. Respect one another and love one another. Soon we were giving advice to others on how we were doing it. We love sharing our story.

> Although we've had our rough patches, we never allowed the rough patches to have us.

I began to share helpful relationship tips on my Facebook page. I saw so many hurting couples it bothered me but I didn't understand why. Meanwhile, my page was growing in numbers. I had over 3,000 people following me on Facebook. A few months before our fifth anniversary, I received a call asking me if I would be willing to come and speak at a marriage retreat. I quickly responded, "YES!!" After I said it, I looked at my wife and said, "What did I just do?" I don't know anything about doing a marriage retreat!!" I began to research like crazy. I really wanted to do this. I felt as if our story could truly help others. On August 24, 2012, we joined my good friend, Pastor Ternae Jordan, Sr. and The Mt. Canaan Baptist Church family at the Winshape Retreat on Berry College Campus in Rome, GA. We had a blast. I did a presentation on the top ten reasons marriages fail. We had couples who had been married a few months to couples who had been together for over forty years. What an impact. Not just my impact on them, but it was their impact on us.

On this trip, Pastor Jordan introduced Deb and I to a man who would push us into our purpose. Dr. David L. Banks. After returning to Chattanooga, we met for lunch and from there, built a bond that is unlike any I have had with a pastor. We later attended his church and began to learn Kingdom principles we had never heard. It was life changing. In December of that year, Dr. Banks did an eight-hour marriage coaching certification class. We jumped at the chance. In this class, we learned some Kingdom principles for marriage that helped us to become even better spouses than before. We learned some tips that challenged us and helped us to improve, but we also learned some things we were already doing really well.

Afterwards, he gave us a test he called "The Purpose Discovery" model. This is a five question test designed to help someone discover their God-Given purpose in life. From that day forward, our lives have not been the same. I learned that my purpose was to help guide others through their relationship challenges; to teach them that a happy, healthy relationship is possible. Deb's purpose was to encourage and empower teens to let them know they can be independent and live a prosperous life. With these tools in place, it was clear what we were designed to do. It's been two years since that took place and we have impacted countless couples, individuals and teens. It is our goal to help others build and maintain healthy relationships. IT IS POSSIBLE!

It is my prayer that my story can help others to overcome the issues that may plague them as it pertains to relationships. I want to be used by God to guide others into the joys of a happy, fulfilling and purpose filled life. I want others to understand IT IS POSSIBLE, but you have to first accept the possibility that maybe the way you have been doing things needs to change. Do what you've never done to get what you've never had. Go where you've never gone to see what you've never seen. Make the changes in your own life that could ultimately redirect your destiny.

# A CHALLENGE TO MY READERS:

**Singles:** Take your time in dating. Don't be led by your flesh or your emotions, but follow the principles of God that will lead you and guide you into the proper position. Remember, blessings come to a position, not a person. Get in Position!

**Engaged Couples:** Invest more in your marriage than you do the wedding. It makes no sense to spend more on a ceremony than you do a lifetime. Premarital doesn't mean talking to someone just before getting married. You may learn some things that let you know that you are not ready to get married. Seek counsel early.

**Married Women:** Encourage your husband. Remind him of his successes more than his failures. Become his biggest cheerleader even when he's sitting on the bench. Your influence can cause him to get into the game and push him to win.

**Married Men:** Keep your wife lifted. Talk to her. Tell her what's on your mind. Communication is key. It builds security for her. She will be willing to follow you anywhere when she's secure in your ability to get her there.

**Married Couples:** If you are struggling in your marriage, seek help. Don't just go to anyone. Be specific. Be intentional. Find someone who can give you more than just knowledge from a book. Be sure they can give you the tools and life lessons to do it the right way.

I am extremely transparent with my life experiences because I believe the only way to truly show someone you understand what they are dealing with is to show them you have been through your own set of issues and have come through them without caving under the pressure. IT IS POSSIBLE to live a fulfilled life. IT IS POSSIBLE to be HAPPILY married. IT IS POSSIBLE to have disagreements that don't become arguments. The reason most of us never achieve this is simply because no one has ever taught us how. Most of us rely more on our own emotions and feelings than we do the application of God's principles.

Marriage is a "God-Ordained" institution and it should not be entered into lightly or without being properly trained or informed. Unfortunately, most go into marriage without setting goals, with little to extremely high and unrealistic expectations, and with their minds more on a fairytale lifestyle than a real life idea about what it means to be married. It is my hope my story will give you some insight on the possibility of real change. I pray my life lessons will inspire you to have a mirror moment. Check yourself to see what it is about you and the decisions you make that leads you to the results you have achieved. Remember, do something different in order to see a different result.

*Interested in booking Eric for speaking engagements, marriage conferences, retreats or singles events?*
*Go to www.realtalkconsultants.com today.*

## ABOUT THE AUTHOR

Eric A. Terry, Sr. is co-owner of RealTalk Consulting. A faith-based firm focused on building and maintaining healthy relationships. He is a Certified Marriage/Relationship Coach under Dr. David L. Banks. He is a licensed minister with over 20 years of experience, as well as a licensed facilitator of the international Prepare/Enrich marriage program. Eric is passionate about helping others navigate the path to healthy relationships. A path that took years for him to discover now expedited for open-minded couples and individuals. Through conferences, private sessions and motivational speaking, Eric is reaching the masses with his message that a happy, healthy relationship is POSSIBLE with the proper tools.

Eric & Deborah Terry

Special thanks: To Nate Cox of Ideal Images Photography and MJT Publishing for his assistance with this project. I could not have done it without you. Thanks for everything!

Check Nate out at:
www.mjtpublishing.com and www.idealimagesphotography.com

---

To Author/Coach Laura Brown, You are a PRICELESS!! Thank you for every bit of advice and encouraging word. You made this process a wonderful journey.

For information on Coach Brown's

Go to www.swatbookcamp.com

For more information and booking, go to www.realtalkconsultants.com or reach Eric via email at info@realtalkconsultants.com

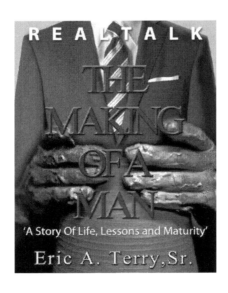

Made in the USA
Lexington, KY
03 January 2015